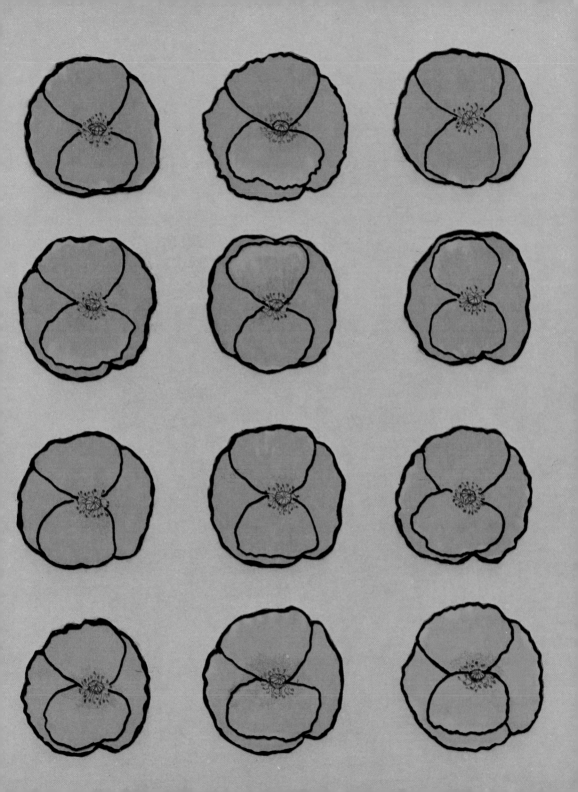

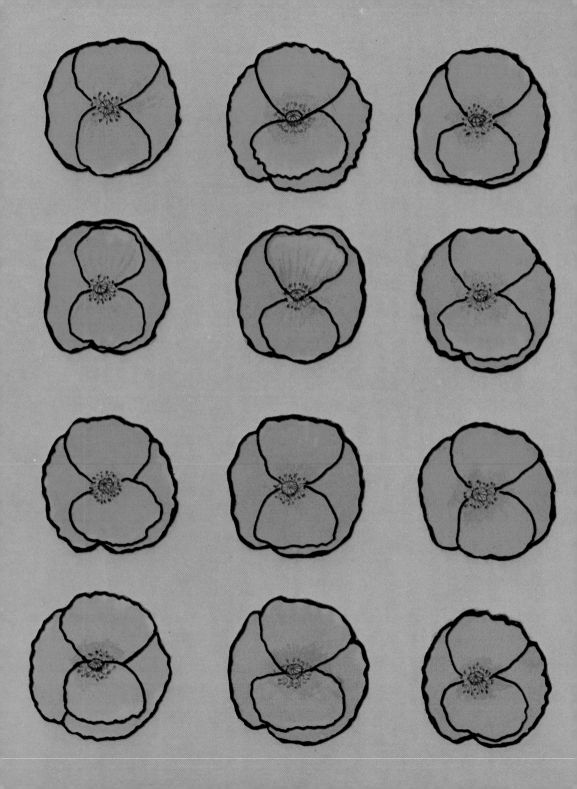

FLOWERS

designed and written by Althea
illustrated by the author

Longman Group USA Inc.

Published in the United States of America by Longman Group USA Inc.
© 1977, 1988 Althea Braithwaite

Originally published in Great Britain in a slightly altered form by Longman Group UK Limited

ISBN: 0-88462-184-7 (library bound)
ISBN: 0-88462-185-5 (paperback)

Printed in the United States of America

88 89 90 10 9 8 7 6 5 4 3 2 1

Library of Congress Cataloging-in-Publication Data

Althea.
   Flowers / designed and written by Althea ; illustrated by the author.
   p.   cm.--(Life-cycle books / Althea)
   Summary: Illustrates how a poppy grows from a seed to a beautiful, red flower.
   1. Flowers--Juvenile literature.   2. Flowers--Life cycle--Juvenile literature.   3.
Poppies--Life cycle--Juvenile literature.   [1. Flowers.   2. Poppies]   I. Title.   II.
Series: Althea.   Life-cycle books.
QK49.A47   1988
582'.0463--dc19   88-8508
ISBN 0-88462-184-7 (lib. bdg.)   CIP
ISBN 0-88462-185-5 (pbk.)   AC

Notes for parents and teachers

Life-Cycle Books have been specially written and designed as a simple, yet informative, series of factual nature books for young children.

The illustrations are bright and clear, and children can "read" the pictures while the story is read to them.

The text has been specially set in large type to make it easy for children to follow along or even to read for themselves.

A plant grows in the field.
It has a strong stem and
green leaves.

At the top of its stem
there is a flower.

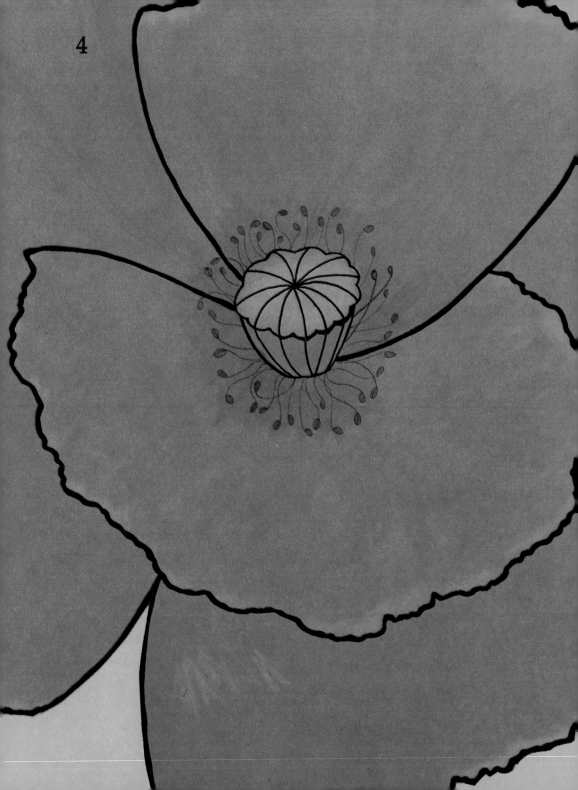

The flower has red petals.
In the middle of the flower
there is a seed box.
It holds many seeds.

This flower needs pollen from another
flower to make the seeds grow.
It is brought by an insect.

The flower's red petals
drop off.
Its leaves turn brown.
Inside the seed box
the tiny seeds are ripe.

The wind shakes the plant
and scatters the seeds
on the ground.

Some of the seeds are
covered by the soil.
During the winter
they do not grow.

In the spring
the sun shines and
warms the soil.

Rains come and it is time
for plants and grass and
trees to grow.
It is time for seeds to sprout.

All winter a hard covering
protected each small,
hidden flower seed.

Now in the damp warm soil,
one seed's hard coat splits.
It sprouts and starts to grow.

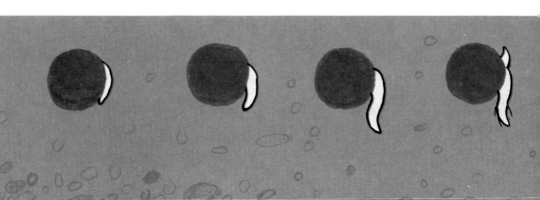

First a root begins to grow.
It goes down into the soil
to get water.

A stem starts to grow, too.
It pokes up and out
of the warm brown soil.

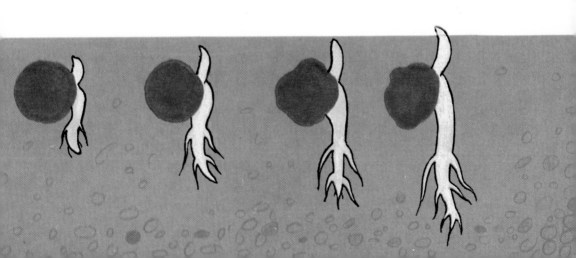

Slowly the plant
grows up through
the soil into
the sunlight and air.

Two green leaves
grow out from
the plant's stem.

The plant gets taller.
Two bigger green leaves
grow from the stem.
Then more leaves grow.

The green leaves need sunshine
and air to make food for the plant.
The roots send water up
through the stem to the leaves.

A green bud grows
at the top of the stem.
Hidden inside the bud
there is a flower
growing.

20

In a few days the bud opens.
Red petals unfold in the
warm sunshine.

The new flower is like
the one that bloomed and
made seeds last summer.

Now the field is filled
with bright red flowers.
Bees fly from flower to flower
collecting sweet nectar.
They carry the pollen dust
from one flower to the next.

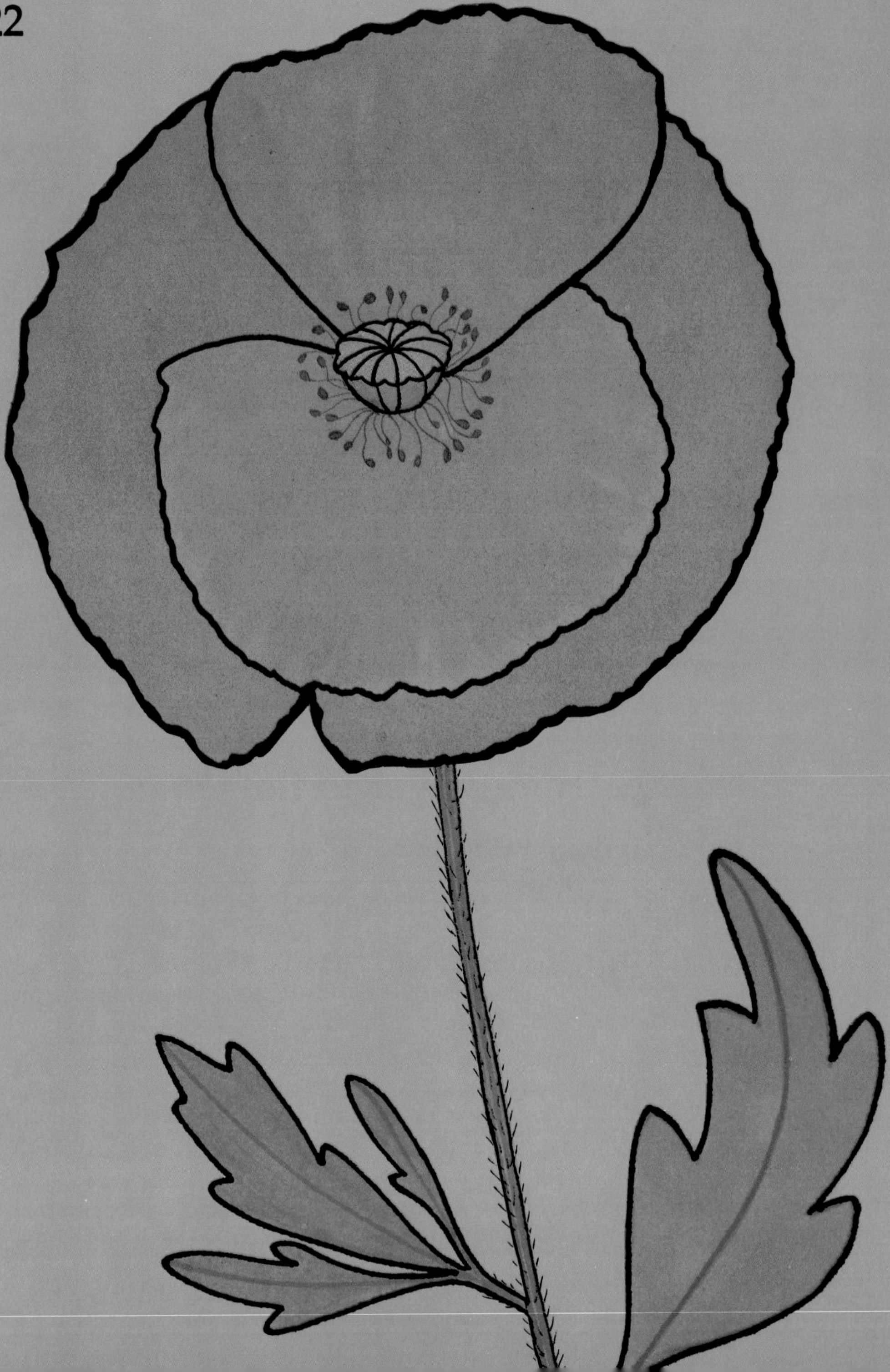

In the middle of the new flower
there is a seed box.
It holds many little seeds.
Next year more red flowers
will bloom here.

FLOWERS and plants are familiar to children at home, in gardens and parks, in fields and along roadsides. Flowers can be planted and their growth observed. It is possible to touch, watch and take them apart to examine. Much of the natural world does not provide so many such direct experiences for child and adult to share.

The cover illustration shows a poppy in full bloom, growing among other plants in a field rather than in a garden. Just as the flower attracts insects to gather pollen, so its brilliant color catches the attention of any passerby. But the flower, once the ovules in its seed capsule have been fertilized, soon dies. While a flower like a poppy has both stamens and pistil, it depends on cross-pollination by insects to produce seeds. This helps ensure a strong new plant.

Poppies can be white, purple, various shades of red and mixed coloring. Among the hundred or so different kinds of poppies, the best known to gardeners is the oriental poppy. As its name suggests, this poppy originated in Asia. It is a spectacular flower, growing on a stalk three to four feet tall.

As children may know, some poppy species are dangerous. But this poppy's ripe seeds are safe to harvest and contain no harmful substances. Poppy seeds are toppings for bread and rolls; crushed, they provide a cooking oil.

People have grown poppies as decorative flowers and for medicinal use for many hundreds of years. Some poppies are annuals, some perennials and some may be both. The handsome oriental poppy is a perennial. Its beauty can dominate a flower bed.

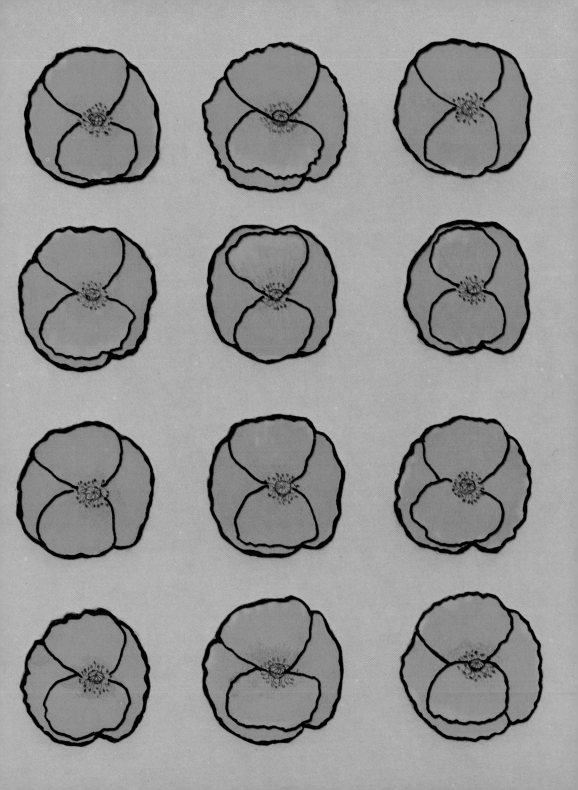

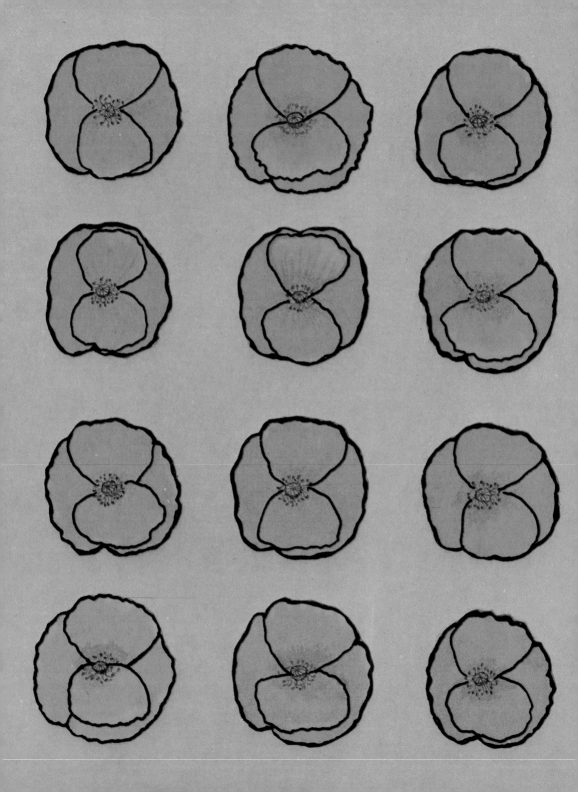